# Favourite Hymns
# We Learned at School

Thomas F. Walsh

ⓔ
MERCIER PRESS

# CONTENTS

# HAIL QUEEN OF HEAVEN

# O COME ALL YE FAITHFUL

## LORD ACCEPT THE GIFTS WE OFFER

## CÉAD MÍLE FÁILTE ROMHAT

## NOW THANK WE ALL OUR GOD

# CREDO IN UNUM DEUM

# INTRODUCTION

When I was growing up in the west of Ireland in the 1950s our world was a very different place from what it is today. It was a simple place, bounded by very identifiable horizons. Our year was marked out by the same feasts and festivals, Christmas and Easter, Advent and Lent. We looked forward to the procession in the town on Corpus Christi, to the Stations in the village, to the Mission when it came to our parish church. We did a Novena to the Holy Souls on the last day of autumn. When we were older we cycled forty miles to Croagh Patrick on the last day of July to climb the holy mountain. We made an annual pilgrimage to Knock and sang hymns to Our Lady.

And the hymns we learned at school were the same hymns our parents had learned. The Mass was the same Latin Mass that had been celebrated for centuries, with the priest facing the altar and the fine old Gregorian chant echoing through the air: 'Credo in unum Deum, Patrem Omnipotentem'. There was a mystery in the Latin and in the Mass, a mystical experience that is missing today.

On Sunday evenings we went to the church for Benediction. We prayed the Rosary and bowed our heads as the monstrance was displayed and we savoured the thick smell of the incense and sang the

'Tantum Ergo' and 'O Salutaris Hostia'.

Then there were special feast-days like St Patrick's Day. We would spend weeks at school learning 'Hail Glorious Saint Patrick' and 'Dóchas Linn Naomh Pádraig' so that we could all troop up the stairs to the organ-loft and join with the choir on that day when we celebrated the national holiday. Inevitably, we would finish off with a resounding rendition of 'Faith of Our Fathers'.

I know from my experience in writing *Favourite Poems We Learned in School* and *More Favourite Poems We Learned in School* that people love to read old poems and songs and hymns not just because they bring them back to their days of innocence and wonder but because they are familiar to them. They are a 'Treasury of the Familiar', as another more famous anthologist put it. Having such a store of well-known and well-loved poetry and music in our possession is a certain security to our spirit in an age of change. Those of us old enough to remember the days when everybody knew the same hymns will find a certain communality here. Who knows, the Church may find that the old hymns that everybody knows are the only ones that will get everybody singing!

I hope you enjoy reading again the hymns you learned at school. I am sure you will find, as I have, that they are powerful and musical and memorable in their own right. They contain the best words in the best order, well constructed and orderly and strong. They have a form and a rhythm and a sequential line of thought. I think they deserve to hold a place in our tradition and I like to think that these hymns we learned at school will never die.

*Thomas F. Walsh, August 1997*

# FAITH OF OUR FATHERS

# FAITH OF OUR FATHERS

Faith of our fathers, living still
In spite of dungeon, fire and sword;
Oh, how our hearts beat high with joy
When e'er we hear that glorious word!

*Chorus*
Faith of our fathers! Holy Faith!
We will be true to thee till death,
We will be true to thee till death.

Our fathers, chained in prisons dark,
Were still in heart and conscience free;
How sweet would be their children's fate,
If they, like them, could die for thee!
*Chorus*

Faith of our fathers, Mary's prayers,
Shall win our country back to thee;
And through the truth that comes from God,
Our land shall then indeed be free.
*Chorus*

Faith of our fathers, we will love
Both friend and foe in all our strife,
And preach thee too, as love knows how,
By kindly words and virtuous life.
*Chorus*

*Frederick William Faber (1814–63)*

# HAIL REDEEMER KING DIVINE

Hail, Redeemer, King divine!
Priest and lamb, the throne is thine,
King whose reign shall never cease,
Prince of everlasting peace.

*Chorus*
Angels, saints and nations sing:
Praised be Jesus Christ, our King:
Lord of life, earth, sky and sea,
King of love on Calvary.

Eucharistic King, what love
Draws thee daily from above,
Clad in signs of bread and wine,
Feed us, lead us, keep us thine.
*Chorus*

King whose name creation thrills,
Rule our minds, our hearts, our wills,
Till in peace each nation rings,
With thy praises, King of kings.
*Chorus*

*Patrick Brennan (1877–1952)*

## Soul of My Saviour

Soul of my Saviour, sanctify my breast;
Body of Christ, be thou my saving guest;
Blood of my Saviour, bathe me in thy tide,
Wash me, ye waters, streaming from his side.

Strength and protection may his passion be:
O blessed Jesus, hear and answer me:
Deep in thy wounds, Lord, hide and shelter me,
So shall I never, never part from thee.

Guard and defend me from the foe malign:
In death's dread moments make me only thine:
Call me, and bid me come to thee on high,
When I may praise thee with thy saints for aye.

*Pope John XXII (1249–1334)*

# O Sacrament Most Holy

O sacrament most holy,
O sacrament divine,
All praise and all thanksgiving
Be ev'ry moment thine.

*Traditional*

## SWEET HEART OF JESUS

Sweet heart of Jesus, fount of love and mercy,
Today we come, thy blessing to implore;
O touch our hearts, so cold and so ungrateful,
And make them, Lord, thine own for evermore.

*Chorus*
Sweet heart of Jesus, we implore,
O make us love thee more and more.

Sweet heart of Jesus, make us pure and gentle,
And teach us how to do thy blessed will;
To follow close the print of thy dear footsteps,
And when we fall – sweet heart, oh, love us still.
*Chorus*

*Sister Marie Josephine SND*

# Sweet Sacrament Divine

Sweet sacrament divine,
Hid in thine earthly home,
Lo! round thy lowly shrine,
With suppliant hearts we come;
Jesus, to thee our voice we raise,
In songs of love and heartfelt praise,
Sweet sacrament divine.

Sweet sacrament of peace,
Dear home of every heart,
Where restless yearnings cease,
And sorrows all depart,
There in thine ear all trustfully
We tell our tale of misery,
Sweet sacrament of peace.

*Francis Stanfield (1835–1914)*

# TO JESUS' HEART ALL BURNING

To Jesus' Heart, all burning
With fervent love for men,
My heart with fondest yearning
Shall raise its joyful strain.

*Chorus*
While ages course along,
Blest be with loudest song
The sacred heart of Jesus
By ev'ry heart and tongue.

O Heart, for me on fire
With love no man can speak,
My yet untold desire
God gives me for thy sake.
*Chorus*

Too true, I have forsaken
Thy love for wilful sin;
Yet now let me be taken
Back by thy grace again.
*Chorus*

As thou are meek and lowly,
And ever pure of heart,
So may my heart be wholly
Of thine the counterpart.
*Chorus*

When life away is flying,
And earth's false glare is done:
Still, sacred Heart, in dying,
I'll say I'm all thine own.
*Chorus*

*Aloys Schlör (1805–52),*
*tr. A. J. Christie SJ*

# HOW GREAT THOU ART

O Lord, my God, when I in awesome wonder,
Consider all the worlds thy hand has made,
I see the stars, I hear the rolling thunder,
Thy pow'r throughout the universe displayed.

*Chorus*
Then sings my soul, my Saviour God, to thee:
How great thou art, how great thou art.
Then sings my soul, my Saviour God, to thee:
How great thou art, how great thou art.

And when I think that God, his Son not sparing,
Sent him to die, I scarce can take it in
That on the cross, my burden gladly bearing,
He bled and died to take away my sin.
*Chorus*

When Christ shall come with shout of acclamation
And take me home, what joy shall fill my heart;
When I shall bow in humble adoration,
And there proclaim: my God, how great thou art.
*Chorus*

> *Anon*

# HOLY GOD WE PRAISE THY NAME

Holy God we praise thy name.
Lord of all we bow before thee.
All on earth thy sceptre own.
All in heaven above adore thee.
Endless is thy vast domain.
Everlasting is thy reign.

Hark, with loud and pealing hymn,
Thee the angel choirs are praising;
Cherubim and seraphim,
One unceasing chorus raising,
Ever sing with sweet accord,
Holy, holy, holy Lord.

Spare thy people, Lord, we pray,
By a thousand snares surrounded:
Keep us free from sin today;
Never let us be confounded.
All my trust I place in thee,
Never, Lord, abandon me.

                    *C. A. Walworth (1820–1900)*

## O God Our Help in Ages Past

O God, our help in ages past,
Our hope for years to come,
Our shelter from the stormy blast,
And our eternal home.

Beneath the shadow of thy throne,
Thy saints have dwelt secure;
Sufficient is thine arm alone,
And our defence is sure.

Before the hills in order stood,
Or earth received her frame,
From everlasting thou art God,
To endless years the same.

A thousand ages in thy sight,
Are like an evening gone;
Short as the watch that ends the night
Before the rising sun.

O God, our help in ages past,
Our hope for years to come,
Be thou our guard while troubles last,
And our eternal home.

*Isaac Watts (1674–1748)*

# TANTUM ERGO

Tantum ergo Sacramentum
veneremur cernui:
et antiquum documentum
novo cedat ritui;
praestet fides supplementum
sensuum defectui.

Genitori, genitoque
laus et jubiliatio,
salus, honor, virtus quoque
sit et benedictio;
procedenti ab utroque
compar sit laudatio.
Amen.

*St Thomas Aquinas (1227–74)*

# O Salutaris Hostia

O salutaris hostia,
quae caeli pandis ostium,
bella premunt hostilia,
da robur, fer auxilium.

Uni trinoque Domino
sit sempiterna gloria,
qui vitam sine termino
nobis donet in patria.
Amen.

*St Thomas Aquinas (1227–74)*

## DÓCHAS LINN NAOMH PÁDRAIG

Dóchas linn Naomh Pádraig, aspal mór na
    hÉireann,
Ainm oirdhearc gléigeal, solas mór and tsaoil é.
D'fhill le sóisceal grá dúinn ainneoin blianta
    'ngéibheann.
Grá mór Mhac na páirte d'fhuascail cách ón
    daorbhroid.

Sléibhte, gleannta, maighe 's bailte mór' na
    hÉireann:
Ghlan sé iad go deo dúinn, míle glóir dár naomh
    dhil.
Iarr'mid ort, a Phádraig, guí orainn na Gaela,
Dia linn lá 'gus oíche 's Pádraig aspal Éireann.

*Traidisiúnta*

# HAIL GLORIOUS SAINT PATRICK

Hail glorious Saint Patrick, dear saint of our isle,
On us thy poor children bestow a sweet smile,
And now thou art high in the mansions above,
On Erin's green valleys look down in thy love.

Ever bless and defend the dear land of our birth,
Where shamrock still blooms as when thou wert
     on earth,
Our hearts shall still burn wheresoever we roam,
For God and Saint Patrick, and our native home.

*Sister Agnes*

# PRAISE MY SOUL THE KING OF HEAVEN

Praise my soul the King of heaven,
To his feet your tribute bring.
Ransomed, healed, restored, forgiven,
Who am I his praise to sing?
Praise him! Praise him! Praise him! Praise him!
Praise the everlasting King!

Praise him for his grace and favour
To our fathers in distress;
Praise him still the same for ever,
Slow to chide and swift to bless.
Praise him! Praise him! Praise him! Praise him!
Glorious in his faithfulness!

Fatherlike, he tends and spares us;
Well our feeble frame he knows;
In his hands he gently bears us,
Rescues us from all our foes.
Praise him! Praise him! Praise him! Praise him!
Widely as his mercy flows!

Angels, help us to adore him;
You behold him face to face;
Sun and moon bow down before him,
Ev'ry thing in time and space.
Praise him! Praise him! Praise him! Praise him!
Praise with us the God of grace!

*Henry Francis Lyte (1793–1847)*

# HAIL QUEEN OF HEAVEN

# HAIL QUEEN OF HEAVEN

Hail, Queen of heav'n, the ocean star,
Guide of the wand'rer here below:
Thrown on life's surge, we claim thy care:
Save us from peril and from woe.
Mother of Christ, star of the sea,
Pray for the wand'rer, pray for me.

O gentle, chaste and spotless maid,
We sinners make our prayers through thee:
Remind thy Son that he has paid
The price of our iniquity.
Virgin most pure, star of the sea,
Pray for the sinner, pray for me.

*John Lingard (1771–1851)*

# THE BELLS OF THE ANGELUS

The bells of the angelus
Call us to pray
In sweet tones announcing
The sacred Ave.

*Chorus*
Ave, Ave, Ave Maria;
Ave, Ave, Ave Maria.

An angel of mercy
Led Bernadette's feet
Where flows the deep torrent
Our Lady to greet.
*Chorus*

She prayed to our mother
That God's will be done,
She prayed for his glory
That his kingdom come.
*Chorus*

Immaculate Mary,
Your praises we sing
Who reign now with Christ,
Our redeemer and king.
*Chorus*

In heaven the blessed
Your glory proclaim,
On earth now your children
Invoke your fair name.
*Chorus*

*Traditional French*

# HOLY MARY FULL OF GRACE

When creation was begun,
God had chosen you to be
Mother of his blessed Son,
Holy Mary, full of grace.

*Chorus*
Ave, Ave, Ave Maria.

When creation was restored,
You were there beside the Lord
Whom you cherished and adored,
Holy Mary, full of grace.
*Chorus*

All of us are children too,
Often doubtful what to do,
Needing to confide in you,
Holy Mary, full of grace.
*Chorus*

You are with us day by day
In our joys and our dismay:
Make us joyful as we say,
'Holy Mary, full of grace.'
*Chorus*

Lady, take us by surprise:
Dazzle our unseeing eyes,
Show us where true beauty lies,
Holy Mary, full of grace.
*Chorus*

Lead us to your child above:
He will teach us how to love,
How to pity and forgive,
Holy Mary, full of grace.
*Chorus*

In the vision which transcends
All our dreams, and never ends,
God will gather all his friends
In the kingdom of your Son.
*Chorus*

Praise the Father and the Son
And the Spirit, three in one,
As it was when time began
Now and evermore. Amen.
*Chorus*

*J.-P. Lecot, tr. Michael Hodgetts*

# I'll Sing a Hymn to Mary

I'll sing a hymn to Mary,
The mother of my God,
The virgin of all virgins,
Of David's royal blood.

*Chorus*
O holy mother Mary,
Ask Christ your Son we pray
To grant us his forgiveness,
And guide us on his way.

Rejoice O holy Mary,
O virgin full of grace,
The Lord is ever with you,
Most blessed of our race.
*Chorus*

*F. Wyse and D. Murray*

# QUEEN OF THE MAY

Bring flowers of the fairest,
Bring blossoms the rarest
From garden and hillside and woodland and dale.
Our full hearts are swelling,
Our glad voices telling
The praise of the loveliest flower of the vale.

*Chorus*
O Mary, we crown thee with blossoms today,
Queen of the Angels and Queen of the May.
O Mary, we crown thee with blossoms again,
Queen of the Angels and Queen of the May.

Their lady they name thee,
Their mistress proclaim thee,
Oh, grant that thy children on earth be as true;
As long as the bowers
Are radiant with flowers,
As long as the azure shall keep its bright hue.
*Chorus*

Sing gaily in chorus,
The bright angels o'er us
Re-echo the strains we begin upon earth;
Their harps are repeating
The notes of our greeting,
For Mary herself is the cause of our mirth.
*Chorus*

Our voices ascending,
In harmony blending,
Oh thus may our hearts turn, dear mother, to thee,
And thus may we prove thee
How truly we love thee,
How dark without Mary life's journey would be.
*Chorus*

> *Traditional*

# AVE MARIA

Ave Maria,
Gratia plena,
Dominus tecum.
Benedicta tu in mulieribus
Et benedictus fructus ventris tui Jesu.

Sancta Maria, Mater Dei,
Ora pro nobis peccatoribus,
Nunc et in hora mortis nostrae.
Amen.

*Traditional (11th century)*

# O PUREST OF CREATURES

O purest of creatures
Sweet mother, sweet maid,
The one spotless womb
Wherein Jesus was laid,
Dark night has come down on us,
Mother, and we
Look out for thy shining, sweet star of the sea.
Sweet star of the sea, sweet star of the sea,
Look out for thy shining, sweet star of the sea.

He gazed on thy soul,
It was sinless and fair;
'Hail, full of grace'
We devoutly declare,
'Conceived without sin'
Thine own title e'er be,
O pray for us who have recourse to thee.
Sweet star of the sea, sweet star of the sea,
O pray for us who have recourse to thee.

*Traditional*

# O Maid Conceived without a Stain

O maid conceived without a stain,
O mother bright and fair,
Come thou within our hearts to reign
And grace shall triumph there.

*Chorus*
Hail Mary ever undefiled,
Hail, Queen of Purity,
O make thy children chaste and mild
And turn their hearts to thee.

O mother of all mothers best
Who soothest every grief,
In thee the weary find the rest
And anguished hearts relief.
*Chorus*

> *Traditional*

# O COME ALL YE FAITHFUL

# O Come All Ye Faithful

O come all ye faithful,
Joyful and triumphant,
O come ye, O come ye to Bethlehem;
Come and behold him,
Born the king of angels.

*Chorus*
O come let us adore him,
O come let us adore him,
O come let us adore him,
Christ the Lord.

Born of the Father,
Light from light eternal,
Son of the gentle maid
Our flesh and blood;
Honour and praise him
With the hosts of angels.
*Chorus*

Sing, choirs of angels,
Sing in exultation,
Sing, all ye citizens of heaven above,
Glory to God
In the highest.
*Chorus*

Now Lord, we greet you,
Born this happy morning,
Jesus to you be glory given,
Word of the Father,
Now in flesh appearing.
*Chorus*

*Traditional, tr. F. Oakeley*

# O COME EMMANUEL

O come, O come, Emmanuel,
To free your captive Israel,
That mourns in lonely exile here,
Until the Son of God appear.

*Chorus*
Rejoice, rejoice, O Israel,
To you shall come Emmanuel.

O royal branch of Jesse's tree,
Redeem us all from tyranny;
From pain of hell your people free,
And over death win victory.
*Chorus*

O come, great daystar, radiance bright,
And heal us with your glorious light.
Disperse the gloomy clouds of night,
And death's dark shadows put to flight.
*Chorus*

O key of David's city, come
And open wide our heav'nly home:
Make safe the way that leads above,
Protect us ever by your love.
*Chorus*

O come, O come, great Lord of might,
Who once appeared on Sinai's height,
And gave your faithful people law,
In all the splendour we adore.
*Chorus*

From the 'Great O Antiphons'
(12th–13th century)
tr. John Mason Neale (1818–66)

## ADESTE FIDELES

Adeste fideles, laeti triumphantes,
Venite, venite in Bethlehem.
Natum videte, regem angelorum,
Venite adoremus, venite adoremus,
Venite adoremus dominum.

Deum de Deo, lumen de lumine,
Gestant puellae viscera.
Deum verum, genitum non factum:
Venite adoremus, venite adoremus,
Venite adoremus dominum.

Cantet nunc Io, chorus angelorum,
Cantet nunc aula caelestium.
Gloria in excelsis Deo,
Venite adoremus, venite adoremus,
Venite adoremus dominum.

Ergo qui natus die hodierna,
Jesu tibi sit gloria.
Patris aeterni Verbum caro factum,
Venite adoremus, venite adoremus,
Venite adoremus dominum.

*Traditional*

## SILENT NIGHT

Silent night, holy night.
All is calm, all is bright
Round yon virgin mother and child;
Holy infant so tender and mild,
Sleep in heavenly peace,
Sleep in heavenly peace.

Silent night, holy night.
Shepherds quake at the sight,
Glories stream from heaven afar,
Heavenly hosts sing alleluia:
Christ the Saviour is born,
Christ the Saviour is born.

Silent night, holy night.
Son of God, love's pure light,
Radiant beams from thy holy face,
With the dawn of redeeming grace,
Jesus, Lord, at thy birth,
Jesus, Lord, at thy birth.

*Joseph Mohr (1792–1848), tr. J. Young*

# Once in Royal David's City

Once in royal David's city
Stood a lowly cattle shed,
Where a mother laid her baby
In a manger for his bed:
Mary was that mother mild,
Jesus Christ her little child.

He came down to earth from heaven
Who is God and Lord of all,
And his shelter was a stable,
And his cradle was a stall;
With the poor, oppressed and lowly
Lived on earth our Saviour holy.

And our eyes at last shall see him,
Through his own redeeming love,
For that child so dear and gentle
Is our Lord in heav'n above;
And he leads his people on
To the place where he is gone.

*Cecil Frances Alexander (1818–95)*

# SEE AMID THE WINTER'S SNOW

See, amid the winter's snow
Born for us on earth below;
See, the tender lamb appears,
Promised from eternal years.

*Chorus*
Hail, thou ever blessed morn.
Hail, redemption's happy dawn.
Sing through all Jerusalem,
Christ is born in Bethlehem.

Lo, within a manger lies
He who built the starry skies;
He who throned in heights sublime
Sits amid the cherubim.
*Chorus*

Say, ye holy shepherds, say,
What's your joyful news today?
Wherefore have ye left your sheep
On the lonely mountain steep?
*Chorus*

'As we watched at dead of night,
Lo, we saw a wondrous light;
Angels, singing peace on earth,
Told us of the Saviour's birth.'
*Chorus*


Sacred infant, all divine,
What a tender love was thine,
Thus to come from highest bliss,
Down to such a world as this.
*Chorus*


Virgin mother, Mary blest,
By the joys that fill thy breast,
Pray for us, that we may prove
Worthy of the Saviour's love.
*Chorus*

*Edward Caswell (1814–78)*

# THE FIRST NOWELL

The first Nowell the angel did say
Was to certain poor shepherds in fields as they lay:
In fields where they lay keeping their sheep,
On a cold winter's night that was so deep.

*Chorus*
Nowell, Nowell, Nowell, Nowell.
Born is the king of Israel!

They looked up and saw a star,
Shining in the east, beyond them far,
And to the earth it gave great light,
And so it continued both day and night.
*Chorus*

And by the light of that same star,
Three wise men came from country far.
To seek for a king was their intent,
And to follow the star wherever it went.
*Chorus*

This star drew nigh to the north-west,
O'er Bethlehem it took its rest,
And there it did both stop and stay,
Right over the place where Jesus lay.
*Chorus*

Then did they know assuredly
Within that house the King did lie:
They entered in then for to see
And found the babe in poverty.
*Chorus*

Then entered in those wise men three,
Full reverently upon their knee,
And offered there in his presence
Their gold and myrrh and frankincense.
*Chorus*

Then let us all with one accord
Sing praises to our heavenly Lord,
That hath made heaven and earth of nought,
And with his blood mankind hath bought.
*Chorus*

*Traditional English*

# HARK THE HERALD ANGELS SING

Hark, the herald angels sing
Glory to the new-born king,
Peace on earth and mercy mild,
God and sinners reconciled:
Joyful all ye nations rise,
Join the triumph of the skies,
With angelic hosts proclaim,
Christ is born in Bethlehem.

*Chorus*
Hark, the herald angels sing
Glory to the new-born king.

Christ, by highest heaven adored,
Christ, the everlasting Lord,
Late in time behold him come,
Offspring of the virgin's womb;
Veiled in flesh the Godhead see;
Hail the incarnate deity,
Pleased as man with man to dwell,
Jesus, our Emmanuel.
*Chorus*

Hail the heaven-born prince of peace.
Hail the son of righteousness.
Light and life to all he brings,
Risen with healing in his wings;
Mild he lays his glory by,
Born that man no more may die,
Born to raise the sons of earth,
Born to give them second birth.
*Chorus*

Charles Wesley (1707–88), G. Whitfield,
Martin Madan (1726–90)

# WHILE SHEPHERDS WATCHED

While shepherds watched their flocks by night,
All seated on the ground,
The angel of the Lord came down,
And glory shone around.

'Fear not,' said he, for mighty dread
Had seized their troubled mind.
'Glad tidings of great joy I bring
To you and all mankind.

'To you in David's town this day
Is born of David's line,
A saviour who is Christ the Lord;
And this shall be the sign:

'The heavenly babe you there shall find
To human view displayed,
All meanly wrapped in swathing bands,
And in a manger laid.'

Thus spoke the Seraph; and forthwith
Appeared a shining throng
Of angels praising God, who thus
Addressed their joyful song:

'All glory be to God on high,
And on the earth be peace;
Good-will henceforth from heaven to men
Begin and never cease.'

*Nahum Tate (1652–1715)*

# ANGELS WE HAVE HEARD ON HIGH

Angels we have heard on high,
Sweetly singing o'er the plains,
And the mountains in reply
Echo still their joyous strains:

*Chorus*
Gloria, in excelsis Deo;
Gloria, in excelsis Deo.

Shepherds, why this jubilee?
Why your rapturous strain prolong?
Say what may your tidings be,
Which inspire your heavenly song.
*Chorus*

Come to Bethlehem and see
Him whose birth the angels sing:
Come, adore on bended knee
Christ our Lord, the new-born king.
*Chorus*

See within a manger laid,
Jesus, Lord of heaven and earth.
Mary, Joseph, lend your aid
To celebrate our Saviour's birth.
*Chorus*

                    *James Chadwick (1813–82)*

# AWAY IN A MANGER

Away in a manger, no crib for a bed,
The little Lord Jesus laid down his sweet head.
The stars in the bright sky looked down where he
     lay,
The little Lord Jesus asleep on the hay.

The cattle are lowing, the baby awakes,
But little Lord Jesus no crying he makes.
I love thee, Lord Jesus! Look down from the sky,
And stay by my side until morning is nigh.

Be near me, Lord Jesus; I ask thee to stay
Close by me for ever, and love me, I pray.
Bless all the dear children in thy tender care,
And fit us for heaven, to live with thee there.
                    *Anon*

# DING DONG MERRILY ON HIGH

Ding dong! merrily on high,
In heav'n the bells are ringing;
Ding dong! verily the sky
Is riv'n with angels singing.

*Chorus*
Gloria, hosanna in excelsis!

E'en so here below, below,
Let steeple bell be swungen,
And io, io, io,
By priest and people sungen.
*Chorus*

Pray you, dutifully prime
Your matin chime, ye ringers;
May you beautifully rhyme
Your eventime song, ye singers.
*Chorus*

*George Ratcliffe Woodward (1848–1934)*

# In the Bleak Midwinter

In the bleak midwinter, frosty wind made moan,
Earth stood hard as iron, water like a stone;
Snow had fallen, snow on snow, snow on snow,
In the bleak midwinter long ago.

Our God, heaven cannot hold him nor earth
    sustain;
Heaven and earth shall flee away, when he comes
    to reign.
In the bleak midwinter, a stable-place sufficed
The Lord God Almighty, Jesus Christ.

Enough for him, whom Cherubim worship night
    and day,
A breastful of milk, and a mangerful of hay:
Enough for him, whom angels fall down before,
The ox and ass and camel which adore.

Angels and archangels may have gathered there;
Cherubim and Seraphim thronged the air.
But only his mother in her maiden bliss
Worshipped the beloved with a kiss.

What can I give him, poor as I am?
If I were a shepherd, I would bring a lamb;
If I were a wise man, I would do my part,
Yet what I can I give him – give my heart.

*Christina Rossetti (1830–94)*

# O LITTLE TOWN OF BETHLEHEM

O little town of Bethlehem,
How still we see thee lie!
Above thy deep and dreamless sleep
The silent stars go by.
Yet, in thy dark streets shineth
The everlasting light;
The hopes and fears of all the years
Are met in thee tonight.

O morning stars, together
Proclaim the holy birth,
And praises sing to God the King,
And peace to men on earth;
For Christ is born of Mary;
And, gathered all above,
While mortals sleep, the angels keep
Their watch of wondering love.

How silently, how silently,
The wondrous gift is given!
So God imparts to human hearts
The blessings of his heaven.
No ear may hear his coming;
But in this world of sin,
Where meek souls will receive him, still
The dear Christ enters in.

Where children pure and happy
Pray to the blessed Child,
Where misery cries out to thee,
Son of the mother mild;
Where charity stands watching
And faith holds wide the door,
The dark night wakes, the glory breaks,
And Christmas comes once more.

*Phillips Brooks (1835–93)*

## WE THREE KINGS

We three kings of Orient are;
Bearing gifts we traverse afar,
Field and fountain, moor and mountain,
Following yonder star.

*Chorus*
O star of wonder, star of night,
Star with royal beauty bright,
Westward leading, still proceeding,
Guide us to thy perfect light.

Born a King on Bethlehem plain,
Gold I bring, to crown him again,
King for ever, ceasing never,
Over us all to reign.
*Chorus*

Frankincense to offer have I,
Incense owns a Deity nigh.
Prayer and praising, all men raising,
Worship him, God most high.
*Chorus*

Myrrh is mine, its bitter perfume
Breathes a life of gathering gloom;
Sorrow sighing, bleeding, dying,
Sealed in the stone-cold tomb.
*Chorus*

Glorious now behold him arise,
King and God and sacrifice;
Alleluia, alleluia,
Earth to heaven replies.
*Chorus*

*John Henry Hopkins (1820–91)*

# LORD ACCEPT THE GIFTS WE OFFER

# LORD ACCEPT THE GIFTS WE OFFER

Lord, accept the gifts we offer
At this Eucharistic feast.
Bread and wine to be transformed now,
Through the action of thy priest.
Take us too Lord, and transform us,
Be thy grace in us increased.

May our souls be pure and spotless
As this host of wheat so fine,
May all stain of sin be crushed out,
Like the grape that forms the wine,
As we, too, become partakers
In this sacrifice divine.

Take our gifts, almighty Father,
Living God, eternal, true,
Which we give, through Christ our Saviour,
Pleading here for us anew.
Grant salvation to all present
And our faith and love renew.

*Sister M. Teresine*

# My God Accept My Heart This Day

My God accept my heart this day,
And make it wholly thine;
That I from thee no more may stray,
No more from thee decline.

Anoint me with thy heavenly grace
And seal me for thine own;
That I may see thy glorious face,
And worship at thy throne.

Let every thought, and work and word
To thee be ever given;
Then life shall be thy service, Lord,
And death the gate of heaven.

All glory to the Father be,
All glory to the Son,
All glory, Holy Ghost, to thee,
While endless ages run.

*Matthew Bridges (1800–94)*

# MEN SOW THE FIELDS IN THE SPRING

Men sow the fields in the spring,
And reap them in the fall;
And from the wheat was made this bread.
We offer it, O Lord.

Men tend the vine in the spring,
And harvest it in the fall;
And from the vine was made this wine.
We offer it, O Lord.

Men cut you down, took your life,
But you arose with the dawn;
And from your death was made our life.
We offer it, O Lord.

*Sean Silke*

# FIRMLY I BELIEVE AND TRULY

Firmly I believe and truly
God is Three, and God is One;
And I next acknowledge duly
Manhood taken by the Son.

And I trust and hope most fully
In that Manhood crucified;
And each thought and deed unruly
Do to death, as he has died.

Simply to his grace and wholly
Light and life and strength belong,
And I love supremely, solely,
Him the holy, him the strong.

And I hold in veneration,
For the love of him alone,
Holy Church as his creation,
And her teachings as his own.

Adoration aye be given,
With and through the angelic host,
To the God of earth and heaven,
Father, Son, and Holy Ghost.

*John Henry Newman (1801–90)*

# WE PLOUGH THE FIELDS AND SCATTER

We plough the fields and scatter
The good seed on the land,
But it is fed and watered
By God's almighty hand;
He sends the snow in winter,
The warmth to swell the grain,
The breezes and the sunshine,
And soft refreshing rain.

*Chorus*
All good gifts around us
Are sent from heav'n above,
Then thank the Lord,
O thank the Lord, for all his love.

He only is the maker
Of all things near and far;
He paints the wayside flower,
He lights the ev'ning star.
The winds and waves obey him,
By him the birds are fed;
Much more to us his children,
He gives our daily bread.
*Chorus*

We thank thee then, O Father,
For all things bright and good;
The seed-time and the harvest,
Our life, our health, our food.
No gifts have we to offer
For all thy love imparts,
But that which thou desirest,
Our humble, thankful hearts.
*Chorus*

> M. *Claudius (1740–1815)*
> *tr. Jane Montgomery Campbell (1817–78)*

# Céad Míle Fáilte Romhat

# CÉAD MÍLE FÁILTE ROMHAT

Céad míle fáilte romhat, a Íosa, a Íosa,
Céad míle fáilte romhat, a Íosa.
Céad míle fáilte romhat, a Shlánaitheoir,
Céad míle míle fáilte romhat, 'Íosa, a Íosa.

Glóir agus moladh duit, a Íosa, a Íosa,
Glóir agus moladh duit, a Íosa.
Glóir agus moladh duit, a Shlánaitheoir,
Glóir, moladh agus buíochas duit, 'Íosa, a Íosa.

*Traidisiúnta*

# COME TO ME LORD

*Chorus*
Come to me Lord, and live within me,
Fill my soul with your life and love.

Free from sin this day, Lord, preserve me,
True to your word give me your peace.
*Chorus*

Bring quick relief to all who suffer,
Comfort and strength to all those who mourn.
*Chorus*

You are the vine, and we the branches,
Though we are many, in you we are one.
*Chorus*

*John V. Moloney*

# CHRIST BE BESIDE ME

Christ be beside me,
Christ be before me,
Christ be behind me,
King of my heart.
Christ be within me,
Christ be below me,
Christ be above me,
Never to part.

Christ on my right hand,
Christ on my left hand,
Christ all around me,
Shield in the strife.
Christ in my sleeping,
Christ in my sitting,
Christ in my rising,
Light of my life.

Christ be in all hearts
Thinking about me,
Christ be on all tongues
Telling of me.
Christ be the vision
In eyes that see me,
In ears that hear me,
Christ ever be.

*Adapted from 'St Patrick's Breastplate'*
*by James Quinn SJ*

# FÁILTE ROMHAT A RÍ NA N-AINGEAL

Fáilte romhat a Rí na n-aingeal,
T'réis do ghlactha, a choirp an Rí;
Fáilte romhat a Rí na bhflaitheas,
Fóir, a Chríost, gach duine dínn.

*Curfá*
Glóir don Athair don Mhac 's don Naoimh-Sprid.
Glóir go deo is moladh síor.

Dia do bheatha, a Thiarna Dia,
Dia is duine thú, a Íosa Críost;
Dia do bheatha, 'bhláth is gile,
Tusa beatha chách go fíor.
*Curfá*

Dia do bheatha, 'bhláth na lile,
'Aon-Mhic Mhuire, a ghin gan smál;
Dia do bheatha, 'chroí is glaine,
D'fhuascail sinn led chrois 's led pháis.
*Curfá*

> *Traidisiúnta*

## COME O CREATOR

Come O Creator Spirit blest,
And in our hearts take up thy rest,
Come with thy grace and heav'nly aid,
To fill the hearts which thou hast made.

Great Paraclete to thee we cry,
O highest gift of God most high,
O fount of life, O fire of love,
And sweet anointing from above.

Drive far from us the foe we dread,
And grant us thy true peace instead.
So shall we not, with thee for guide,
Turn from the path of life aside.

All glory while the ages run,
Be to the Father and the Son,
Who rose from death; the same to thee,
O Holy Ghost, eternally.

*Edward Caswell (1814–78)*

## Veni Creator Spiritus

Veni, Creator Spiritus
mentes tuorum visita,
imple superna gratia,
quae tu creasti pectora.

Qui diceris Paraclitus,
Altissimi donum Dei,
fons vivus, ignis, caritas,
et spiritalis unctio.

Tu septiformis munere,
digitus paternae dexterae.
Tu rite promissum Patris,
sermone ditans guttura.

Accende lumen sensibus,
infunde amorem cordibus,
infirma nostri corporis
virtute firmans perpeti.

Hostem repellas longius,
pacemque dones protinus:
ductore sic te praevio,
vitemus omne noxium.

Per te sciamus, da, Patrem,
noscamus atque Filium,
teque utriusque Spiritum
credamus omni Tempore.

Deo Patri sit gloria,
et Filio, qui a mortuis
surrexit, ac Paraclito,
in saeculorum saecula.
Amen.

*Attributed to Rabanus Maurus (766–856)*

# THE KING OF LOVE

The King of love my Shepherd is,
Whose goodness faileth never;
I nothing lack if I am his
And he is mine for ever.

Where streams of living water flow
My ransomed soul he leadeth,
And where the verdant pastures grow
With food celestial feedeth.

Perverse and foolish oft I strayed,
But yet in love he sought me,
And on his shoulder gently laid,
And home, rejoicing, brought me.

In death's dark vale I fear no ill
With thee, dear Lord, beside me;
Thy rod and staff my comfort still,
Thy cross before to guide me.

Thou spread'st a table in my sight,
Thy unction grace bestoweth:
And O what transport of delight
From thy pure chalice floweth!

And so through all the length of days
Thy goodness faileth never;
Good Shepherd, may I sing thy praise
Within thy house for ever.

*Henry Williams Baker (1821–77)*

# NOW THANK WE ALL OUR GOD

# NOW THANK WE ALL OUR GOD

Now thank we all our God,
With heart and hands and voices,
Who wondrous things has done,
In whom the world rejoices;
Who from our mother's arms
Has blessed us on our way
With countless gifts of love,
And still is ours today.

O may this bounteous God
Through all our lives be near us,
With ever joyful hearts
And blessed peace to cheer us;
And keep us in his grace,
And guide us when perplexed,
And free us from all ills
In this world and the next.

All praise and thanks to God
The Father now be given,
The Son and Spirit blest
Who reign in highest heaven,
The one Eternal God,
Whom earth and heaven adore;
For thus it was, is now,
And shall be evermore.

*Martin Rinkart (1586–1649),*
*tr. Catherine Winkworth (1829–78)*

## LORD OF ALL HOPEFULNESS

Lord of all hopefulness, Lord of all joy,
Whose trust, ever childlike, no cares could destroy,
Be there at our waking, and give us, we pray,
Your bliss in our hearts, Lord, at the break of the
    day.

Lord of all eagerness, Lord of all faith,
Whose strong hands were skilled at the plane and
    the lathe,
Be there at our labours, and give us, we pray,
Your strength in our hearts, Lord, at the noon of the
    day.

Lord of all kindliness, Lord of all grace,
Your hands swift to welcome, your arms to embrace,
Be there at our homing, and give us, we pray,
Your love in our hearts, Lord, at the eve of the day.

Lord of all gentleness, Lord of all calm,
Whose voice is contentment, whose presence is balm,
Be there at our sleeping, and give us, we pray,
Your peace in our hearts, Lord, at the end of the day.

*Jan Struther (1901–53)*

# ALL PEOPLE THAT ON EARTH

All people that on earth do dwell,
Sing to the Lord with cheerful voice;
Serve him with gladness, praise him well:
Come now before him and rejoice.

Know that the Lord is God indeed,
In his great love created man:
God is our shepherd, every need
He has supplied since time began.

Enter his gates with songs of praise,
Come to his courts, approach with joy:
Honour and bless him all our days,
Gladly for God our lives employ.

Truly, the Lord our God is good,
His mercy is for ever sure:
His truth at all times firmly stood
And shall from age to age endure.

*Adapted from Psalm 100*
*by William Kethe (?–1594)*

## Amazing Grace

Amazing grace! How sweet the sound
That saved a wretch like me.
I once was lost but now I'm found,
Was blind, but now I see.

'Twas grace that taught my heart to fear,
And grace my fears relieved.
How precious did that grace appear
The hour I first believed.

Through many dangers, toils and snares
I have already come.
'Tis grace hath brought me safe thus far,
And grace will lead me home.

The Lord has promised good to me;
His word my hope secures.
He will my shield and portion be
As long as life endures.

*John Newton (1725–1807)*

# NEARER MY GOD TO THEE

Nearer my God to thee, nearer to thee.
E'en though it be a cross that raiseth me:
Still all my song shall be, nearer my God to thee,
Nearer my God to thee, nearer to thee.

Though like the wanderer, the sun gone down,
Darkness be over me, my rest a stone:
Yet in my dreams I'd be nearer my God to thee,
Nearer my God to thee, nearer to thee.

There let the way appear steps unto heav'n:
All that thou sendest me in mercy giv'n:
Angels to beckon me nearer my God to thee,
Nearer my God to thee, nearer to thee.

Deep in thy sacred heart let me abide,
Thou who hast come for me, suffered and died.
Sweet shall my weeping be, grief surely leading me
Nearer my God to thee, nearer to thee.

*Sarah Flower Adams (1805–48)*

# THE BATTLE-HYMN OF THE REPUBLIC

Mine eyes have seen the glory of the coming of
    the Lord.
He is tramping out the vintage where the grapes of
    wrath are stored.
He has loosed the fateful lightning of his terrible
    swift sword.
His truth is marching on.

*Chorus*
Glory, glory halleluja!
Glory, glory halleluja!
Glory, glory halleluja!
His truth is marching on.

I have seen him in the watchfires of a hundred
    circling camps.
They have gilded him an altar in the evening dews
    and damps.
I can read his righteous sentence by the dim and
    flaring lamps.
His day is marching on.
*Chorus*

He has sounded forth the trumpet that shall never
   sound retreat.
He is sifting out the hearts of men before his
   judgement seat.
O, be swift my soul to answer him, be jubilant my
   feet!
Our God is marching on.
*Chorus*

In the beauty of the lilies Christ was born across
   the sea
With a glory in his bosom that transfigures you
   and me.
As he died to make men holy, let us die to make
   men free.
Whilst God is marching on.
*Chorus*

*Julia Ward Howe (1819–1910)*

# LEAD KINDLY LIGHT

Lead, kindly light amid th'encircling gloom,
Lead thou me on;
The night is dark, and I am far from home,
Lead thou me on.
Keep thou my feet; I do not ask to see
The distant scene; one step enough for me.

I was not ever thus, nor prayed that thou
Shouldst lead me on;
I loved to choose and see my path; but now
Lead thou me on.
I loved the garish day, and, spite of fears,
Pride ruled my will; remember not past years.

So long thy power hath blest me, sure it still
Will lead me on
O'er moor and fen, o'er crag and torrent, till
The night is gone,
And with the morn those angel faces smile
Which I have loved long since, and lost awhile.

*John Henry Newman (1801–90)*

# ALL THINGS BRIGHT AND BEAUTIFUL

*Chorus*
All things bright and beautiful,
All creatures great and small,
All things wise and wonderful,
The Lord God made them all.

Each little flower that opens,
Each little bird that sings,
He made their glowing colours,
He made their tiny wings.
*Chorus*

The purple-headed mountain,
The river running by,
The sunset and the morning,
That brightens up the sky.
*Chorus*

The cold wind in the winter,
The pleasant summer sun,
The ripe fruits in the garden,
He made them every one.
*Chorus*

The tall trees in the greenwood,
The meadows for our play,
The rushes by the water,
We gather every day.
*Chorus*

He gave us eyes to see them,
And lips that we may tell
How great is God Almighty,
Who has made all things well.
*Chorus*

*Cecil Frances Alexander (1818–95)*

# PRAISE TO THE LORD

Praise to the Lord, the Almighty, the king of
  creation.
O my soul praise him for he is your health and
  salvation.
All you who hear, now to his altar draw near,
Joining in glad adoration.

Praise to the Lord, let us offer our gifts at his
  altar:
Let not our sins and transgressions now cause us
  to falter.
Christ the high priest bids us all join in his feast,
Victims with him on the altar.

Praise to the Lord, who will prosper our work and
  defend us:
Surely his goodness and mercy here daily attend
  us:
Ponder anew all the Almighty can do,
He who with love will befriend us.

Praise to the Lord, oh let all that is in us adore
him!
All that has life and breath, come now in praises
before him.
Let the Amen sound from his people again,
Now as we worship before him.

*Joachim Neander (1650–80)*
*tr. Catherine Winkworth (1829–78)*

## The Lord's My Shepherd

The Lord's my shepherd, I'll not want.
He makes me down to lie
In pastures green, he leadeth me
The quiet waters by.

My soul he doth restore again,
And me to walk doth make
Within the paths of righteousness,
E'en for his own name's sake.

Yea, though I walk through death's dark vale,
Yet will I fear no ill;
For thou art with me, and thy rod
And staff me comfort still.

My table thou hast furnished
In presence of my foes:
My head thou dost with oil anoint,
And my cup overflows.

Goodness and mercy all my life
Shall surely follow me:
And in God's house for evermore
My dwelling-place shall be.

*Paraphrased from Psalm 22*
*in the* Scottish Psalter *(1650)*

# A Íosa Glan Mo Chroíse

A Íosa glan mo chroíse
Go gléghlan gach lá;
A Íosa cuir m'intinn
Faoi léirsmacht do ghrá.

Déan mo smaointe go fíorghlan
Agus briathra mo bhéil,
'S a Thiarna, 'Dhia dhílis,
Stiúraigh choíche mo shaol.

*Traidisiúnta*

# ABIDE WITH ME

Abide with me, fast falls the eventide;
The darkness deepens, Lord, with me abide!
When other helpers fail, and comforts flee,
Help of the helpless, O abide with me.

Swift to its close ebbs out life's little day;
Earth's joys grow dim, its glories pass away;
Change and decay in all around I see;
O thou who changest not, abide with me.

I need thy presence every passing hour;
What but thy grace can foil the tempter's power?
Who like thyself my guide and stay can be?
Through cloud and sunshine, O abide with me.

I fear no foe with thee at hand to bless;
Ills have no weight, and tears no bitterness.
Where is death's sting? Where, grave, thy victory?
I triumph still, if thou abide with me.

Hold thou thy Cross before my closing eyes;
Shine through the gloom, and point me to the
        skies;
Heaven's morning breaks, and earth's vain shadows
        flee:
In life, in death, O Lord, abide with me!

*Henry Francis Lyte (1793–1847)*

# CREDO IN UNUM DEUM

# KYRIE

Kyrie, eleison.
Kyrie, eleison.
Christe, eleison.
Christe, eleison.
Kyrie, eleison.
Kyrie, eleison.

# GLORIA

Gloria in excelsis Deo
et in terra pax hominibus bonae voluntatis.
Laudamus te,
benedicimus te,
adoramus te,
glorificamus te,
gratias agimus tibi propter magnam
gloriam tuam,
Domine Deus, Rex caelestis,
Deus Pater omnipotens.
Domine Fili unigenite, Jesu Christe,
Domine Deus, Agnus Dei, Filius Patris,
qui tollis peccata mundi, miserere nobis;
qui tollis peccata mundi,
suscipe deprecationem nostram;
qui sedes ad dexteram Patris, miserere nobis.
Quoniam tu solus Sanctus, tu solus Dominus,
tu solus Altissimus,
Jesu Christe, cum Sancto Spiritu: in gloria Dei Patris.
Amen.

# CREDO

Credo in unum Deum,
Patrem Omnipotentem, factorem caeli et terrae,
visibilium omnium et invisibilium.
Et in unum Dominum Jesum Christum,
Filium Dei unigenitum,
et ex Patre natum ante omnia saecula.
Deum de Deo, lumen de lumine,
Deum verum de Deo vero,
genitum, non factum, consubstantialem Patri:
per quem omnia facta sunt.
Qui propter nos homines
et propter nostram salutem
descendit de caelis.
Et incarnatus est de Spiritu Sancto
ex Maria Virgine, et homo factus est.
Crucifixus etiam pro nobis sub Pontio Pilato;
passus et sepultus est,
et resurrexit tertia die, secundum Scripturas,
et ascendit in caelum, sedet ad dexteram Patris.
Et iterum venturus est cum gloria,
iudicare vivos et mortuos,
cuius regni non erit finis.
Et in Spiritum Sanctum, Dominum et
vivificantem:
qui ex Patre Filioque procedit.
Qui cum Patre et Filio simul adoratur et

conglorificatur:
qui locutus est per prophetas.
Et unam, sanctam, catholicam
et apostolicam Ecclesiam.
Confiteor unum baptisma in remissionem
peccatorum.
Et exspecto resurrectionem mortuorum,
et vitam venturi saeculi.
Amen.

## SANCTUS

Sanctus, Sanctus, Sanctus Dominus Deus Sabaoth.
Pleni sunt caeli et terra gloria tua.
Hosanna in excelsis.
Benedictus qui venit in nomine Domini.
Hosanna in excelsis.

## PATER NOSTER

Pater noster, qui es in caelis:
sanctificetur nomen tuum;
adveniat regnum tuum;
fiat voluntas tua, sicut in caelo, et in terra.

Panem nostrum cotidianum da nobis hodie;
et dimitte nobis debita nostra,
sicut et nos dimittimus debitoribus nostris;
et ne nos inducas in tentationem;
sed libera nos a malo.
Amen.

# AGNUS DEI

Agnus Dei, qui tollis peccata mundi:
miserere nobis.
Agnus Dei, qui tollis peccata mundi:
miserere nobis.
Agnus Dei, qui tollis peccata mundi:
dona nobis pacem.

# INDEX OF AUTHORS

# Index of Titles

# INDEX OF FIRST LINES

# ACKNOWLEDGEMENTS

The editor and publishers are grateful to the following, who kindly gave permission for copyright material to be included in this book:

Geoffrey Chapman, an imprint of Cassell, Wellington House, 125 Strand, London WC2R OBB. for 'Christ Be Beside Me' © James Quinn SJ.

Michael Hodgetts for 'Holy Mary Full of Grace' translated by Michael Hodgetts.

Monsignor John V. Moloney for 'Come to Me Lord' by John V. Moloney.

Bishop Donal Murray for 'Hail Glorious Saint Patrick' by Sister Agnes and 'I'll Sing a Hymn to Mary' by F. Wyse and D. Murray

Oxford University Press for 'Lord of All Hopefulness' by Jan Struther (1901–53) © 1931 from *Enlarged Songs of Praise*.

Every attempt has been made to get in touch with copyright holders. The publishers will be glad to come to an arrangement with any copyright holders whom it has not been possible to reach.